Button, Button,

Who's Got the Button?

Trish Holland

TeachingStrategies • Washington D.C.

For Teaching Strategies, Inc.
Publisher: Larry Bram
Editorial Director: Hilary Parrish Nelson
VP Curriculum and Assessment: Cate Heroman
Product Manager: Kai-leé Berke
Book Development Team: Sherrie Rudick and Jan Greenberg
Project Manager: Jo A. Wilson

For Q2AMedia
Editorial Director: Bonnie Dobkin
Editor and Curriculum Adviser: Suzanne Barchers
Program Manager: Gayatri Singh
Creative Director: Simmi Sikka
Project Manager: Santosh Vasudevan
Designers: Ritu Chopra & Shruti Aggarwal
Picture Researcher: Anita Gill

Picture Credits
t-top b-bottom c-center l-left r-right

Cover: Kiselev Andrey Valerevich/Shutterstock.

Back Cover: Kate Leigh/Istockphoto: tl, Kate Leigh/Istockphoto: tr,
Kate Leigh/Istockphoto: c, Kate Leigh/Istockphoto: b.

Title Page: KL Photography/Istockphoto.

Insides: Ryan Lane/Istockphoto, David Hernandez/Dreamstime:
3, Hughestoneian/Dreamstime: 3/Istockphoto: 4, Kiselev Andrey
Valerevich/Shutterstock: 5, 123RF: 6, Q2AMedia Image Bank:
7, Uzumba/Fotolia: 8, Masterfile: 9, Juliya Baranova/Fotolia:
10, Jennifer Photography & Imaging/Shutterstock: 11, Benjamin
O'Neal/Istockphoto: 12, Vyacheslav Osokin/Shutterstock: 13,
Raja Rc/Dreamstime: 14, Glow Images/Photolibrary: 15, Photo
25th/Dreamstime: 16, Glue Stock/Shutterstock: 17l, Andrew
Manley/Istockphoto: 17r, Bakaleev Aleksey/Istockphoto: 18,
Image100 Limited/Photolibrary: 19, Elena Rachkovskaya/123RF:
20, Petrenko Andriy/Shutterstock: 21, Thomas M Perkins/
Shutterstock: 22, Q2AMedia Image Bank: 23tl, Jennifer
Photography & Imaging/Istockphoto: 23tr, Image100 Limited/
Photolibrary: 23bl, Glow Images/Photolibrary : 23br, Matka
Wariatka/Shutterstock: 24.

Teaching Strategies, Inc.
P.O. Box 42243
Washington, DC 20015
www.TeachingStrategies.com

ISBN: 978-1-60617-118-9

Library of Congress Cataloging-in-Publication Data
Holland, Trish.
  Button, button, who's got the button? / Trish Holland.
    p. cm.
  ISBN 978-1-60617-118-9
  1. Clothing and dress--Juvenile literature. 2. Fasteners--Juvenile literature. I. Title.
  GT518.H64 2010
  391--dc22
                        2009036780
CPSIA tracking label information:
RR Donnelley, Shenzhen, China
Date of Production: June 2014
Cohort: Batch 3

Printed and bound in China

5 6 7 8 9 10	15 14
Printing	Year Printed

Button, button,
who's got the button?

How many buttons
do you have?

Button, button,
I've got

one
button.

A big button
brightening
my cape!

1

Buckle, buckle,
who's got the buckle?

How many buckles
do you have?

Buckle, buckle,
we've got **two** buckles.
Bold buckles bumping on our belts.

2

Knot, knot,
who's got the knot?

How many knots
do you have?

Knot, knot,
we've got **three** knots.

Nimble knots nipping at our necks.

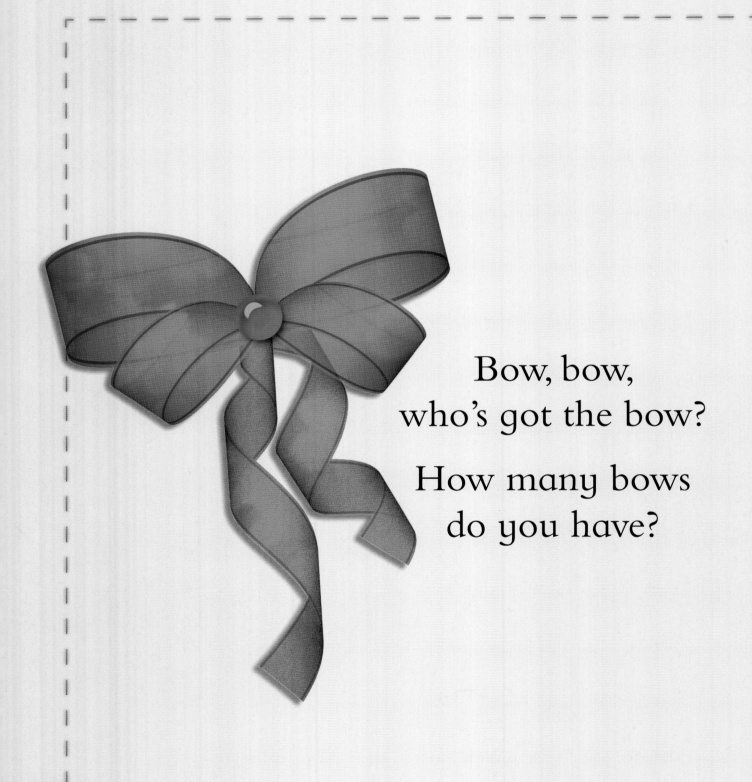

3

Bow, bow,
who's got the bow?

How many bows
do you have?

4

Bow, bow,
we've got **four** bows.
Bashful bows blooming on our backs.

Loop, loop,
who's got loops?

How many loops
do you have?

5

Loop, loop,
I've got **five** loops.

Long loops locking out the cold.

Zipper, zipper,
who's got the zipper?

How many zippers
do you have?

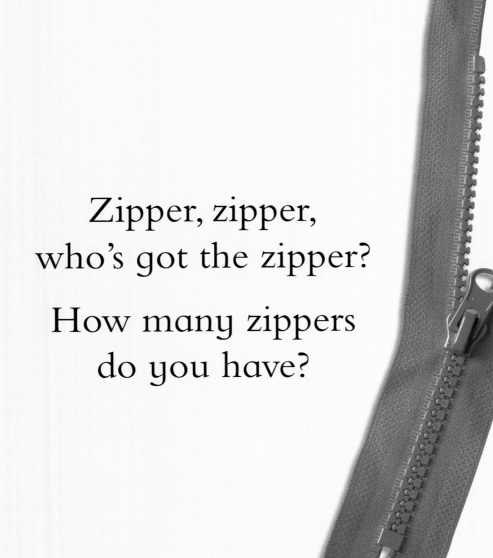

Zipper, zipper,
we've got **six** zippers.

Zany zippers zooming on our coats.

Toggle, toggle,
who's got the toggle?

How many toggles
do you have?

Toggle, toggle,
we've got **seven** toggles.
Tricky toggles tilting to and fro.

Shoelace, shoelace, who's got the shoelace?

How many laces do you have?

Shoelace, shoelace,
we've got **eight** shoelaces.
Lazy laces looping along our feet.

8

Snap, snap,
who's got the snap?

How many snaps
do you have?

9

Snap, snap,
I've got
nine
snaps.

Silly snaps
snicking
as they shut.

10

And
button, button,
I've got

ten

buttons.
A bunch of buttons
boasting
we're the best!

Many ways to close our clothing:
Buttons, buckles, loops, and bows,
Toggles, zippers, knots, and snaps,
Lots of laces, and who knows…?

Can you
find one
more?